First World War
and Army of Occupation
War Diary
France, Belgium and Germany

74 (YEOMANRY) DIVISION
230 Infantry Brigade
Royal Sussex Regiment
16th Battalion
1 May 1918 - 31 May 1919

WO95/3153/4

The Naval & Military Press Ltd
www.nmarchive.com
Published in association with The National Archives

Published by

The Naval & Military Press Ltd

Unit 10 Ridgewood Industrial Park,

Uckfield, East Sussex,

TN22 5QE England

Tel: +44 (0) 1825 749494

www.naval-military-press.com

www.nmarchive.com

This diary has been reprinted in facsimile from the original. Any imperfections are inevitably reproduced and the quality may fall short of modern type and cartographic standards.

© **Crown Copyright**
Images reproduced by permission of The National Archives, London, England, 2015.

Contents

Document type	Place/Title	Date From	Date To
Heading	WO95/3153/4 16 Battalion Royal Sussex Reg		
Heading	230th Brigade 74th Division France 16th Battalion Royal Sussex Regt. 1918 May-1919 Apl		
Miscellaneous	War Diary For The Month of May	31/05/1918	31/05/1918
Heading	230th Brigade 74th Division France 16th Battalion Royal Sussex Regt. Jan-Apr 1919		
War Diary	Alexandria	01/05/1918	01/05/1918
War Diary	At Sea	02/05/1918	06/05/1918
War Diary	Marseilles	07/05/1918	12/05/1918
War Diary	Morlay	13/05/1918	22/05/1918
War Diary	Foufflin Ricametz	23/05/1918	25/05/1918
War Diary	Manin	26/05/1918	25/06/1918
War Diary	Flechin	26/06/1918	10/07/1918
War Diary	Guarbecque	11/07/1918	12/07/1918
War Diary	In The Line	13/07/1918	23/07/1918
War Diary	Guarbecque	24/07/1918	04/08/1918
War Diary	In The Line	05/08/1918	16/08/1918
War Diary	Hamet Billet	17/08/1918	26/08/1918
War Diary	Bourecq	27/08/1918	29/08/1918
War Diary	Heilly	30/08/1918	31/08/1918
War Diary	Hem Wood	01/09/1918	02/09/1918
War Diary	Trenches SE Of Haute Allaines	03/09/1918	04/09/1918
War Diary	In Bivouac At C.26.a & C	05/09/1918	05/09/1918
War Diary	Aizecourt D.26.c	06/09/1918	06/09/1918
War Diary	Templeux La Fosse	07/09/1918	07/09/1918
War Diary	E.26.b.	08/09/1918	10/09/1918
War Diary	Spur Quarry	11/09/1918	18/09/1918
War Diary	Sherwood Trench	19/09/1918	19/09/1918
War Diary	Templeux Switch	20/09/1918	21/09/1918
War Diary	Toine Post	22/09/1918	23/09/1918
War Diary	Sherwood Trench	24/09/1918	24/09/1918
War Diary	Templeux Le Fosse	25/09/1918	25/09/1918
War Diary	Fouilloy	26/09/1918	30/09/1918
War Diary	Le Cleme	01/10/1918	01/10/1918
War Diary	Richbourg	02/10/1918	02/10/1918
War Diary	Halpegarbe	03/10/1918	03/10/1918
War Diary	Le Cocquerez Farm	04/10/1918	09/10/1918
War Diary	Chateau de la Vallee	10/10/1918	16/10/1918
War Diary	Flequiries	17/10/1918	17/10/1918
War Diary	Ronchin	18/10/1918	18/10/1918
War Diary	Chereng	19/10/1918	19/10/1918
War Diary	Camphim	20/10/1918	24/10/1918
War Diary	Marquain	25/10/1918	30/10/1918
War Diary	Lemain	31/10/1918	09/11/1918
War Diary	Tournai	10/11/1918	11/11/1918
War Diary	Montroeul Bois	12/11/1918	12/11/1918
War Diary	Sartiau	13/11/1918	13/11/1918
War Diary	Pironche	16/11/1918	16/11/1918
War Diary	Thimougies	17/11/1918	15/12/1918
War Diary	Frasnes	16/12/1918	16/12/1918

War Diary	Ogy	17/12/1918	17/12/1918
War Diary	Bievene	18/12/1918	27/02/1919
War Diary	Grammont	28/02/1919	01/04/1919
War Diary	Grammont Belgium	01/04/1919	31/05/1919

Wol 95 B 153/4

16 Buttatia Royale Sussex Reg.

230TH BRIGADE
74TH DIVISION

FRANCE
16TH BATTALION
ROYAL SUSSEX REGT.
~~MAY – DEC 1918~~
~~JAN – APR 1919~~

1918 MAY — 1919 APL

SECRET.

From: O.C.
(Sx. Yeo.) Battn.
Royal Sussex Regt.

No: M 2
230th May

Herewith War Diary
for the month of May.

[signature]
Major
31.5.18.   Cmdg. (Sx. Yeo.) Battn.
                                        Royal Sussex Regt.

230TH BRIGADE
74TH DIVISION

FRANCE

16TH BATTALION

ROYAL SUSSEX REGT.

JAN - APR 1919

May 1/18
16 R Sussex R

Army Form C. 2118

WAR DIARY
or
INTELLIGENCE SUMMARY
(Erase heading not required.)

Instructions regarding War Diaries and Intelligence Summaries are contained in F. S. Regs., Part II. and the Staff Manual respectively. Title Pages will be prepared in manuscript.

Place	Date 1918	Hour	Summary of Events and Information	Remarks and references to Appendices
ALEXANDRIA	May 1st		Sailed from ALEXANDRIA on H.M.T. "CALEDONIA" at sea.	
AT SEA	2-6			
MARSEILLES	7,8		Arrived MARSEILLES turned into camp at No 10 Rest Camp	
	9		Entrained for the north on the train.	
	10,11		Arrived at NOYELLE and went into billets as follows:-	
	12		H.Q., A Coy, B Coy (less 1 platoon) at MORLANCOURT. HAMEL. C Coy - PONTHOILE. D Coy & 1 platoon B Coy	
MORLANCOURT	13-21		Training & re-organising - Refugees on Gas and Bayonet fighting	
	22		Entrained at RUE for LIGNY ST FLOCHEL and went into Billets at TOUFFLIN RICAMETZ	
TOUFFLIN RICAMETZ	23,24		Remained in Billets	
	25		Marched to & went into Billets at NANIX	6
NANIX	26,27		Training	3
	28		XV Battalion were inspected by G.O.C. 74th (Yeo) Division	
	29-31		Training	
			General Notes.	
			The Health of the troops extremely generally good but have been abnormal cases of Colds & flues as a result of the change of climate	
			Reinforcements.	
			Officers 2 Other Ranks 7	
			Effective Strength.	
			Officers 41 Other Ranks 950	

[Signed] ......
Major
C.O. 16 (Sx Yeo) Batt.
Royal Sussex Regt.

16th (Sx) Regiment R——

Army Form C. 2118.
JUNE 1918

WAR DIARY
or
INTELLIGENCE SUMMARY.
(Erase heading not required.)

Instructions regarding War Diaries and Intelligence
Summaries are contained in F.S. Regs., Part II.
and the Staff Manual respectively. Title pages
will be prepared in manuscript.

Place	Date 1918	Hour	Summary of Events and Information	Remarks and references to Appendices
MANIN	June 1st-24th	—	The Battalion carried out open warfare training, including practice attack with Tanks. Throughout this period.	
	25th		The Battalion moved NORTH going into billets in FLECHIN	
FLECHIN	26th-30th	—	The Battalion continued open warfare training.	
			Reinforcements during Month 4 Officers 119 Other Ranks Effective Strength 43 Officers 920 Other Ranks	
			The health of the troops on the whole continued to be good throughout the month but since moving to FLECHIN several cases of Three days fever occurred and the complaints appears to be largely on the increase.	

A. Miller
Capt. & Adjt.

YEOMANRY BATT.
Royal Sussex Regiment

Army Form C. 2118.

WAR DIARY
or
INTELLIGENCE SUMMARY.

(Erase heading not required.)

16th Reserve Regt
July 1-16

Place	Date	Hour	Summary of Events and Information	Remarks and references to Appendices
FLECHIN	July 1-9		Training continued throughout this period	
	10th		Battalion moved to and went into billets at GUARBECQUE	
GUARBECQUE	11-12		The Battalion went into the line and relieved the 2/7 R.WARWICK REGIMENT in the left sub section of the ROEBECQ Sector, holding the front line from Q.11.a.2.9 to Q.8.a.0.3. Battalion Headquarters at LES AMUSOIRES, two Companies in the front line, A Coy (Capt LASCELLES) on the right, B Coy (Lieut ADAMS) on the left, D Coy (Capt CUTHBERTSON) in support, C Coy (Capt T.A.R.EDWARDS) in reserve. 15th SUFFOLKS holding the right sub section, with 10th BUFFS as Brigade reserve. The relief was carried out without incident and the Battalion only had one Casualty during the	
IN THE LINE	13-14		" " of the relief. The Battalion remained in the line. 2/Lt C.T.BASS wounded on patrol night inst.	
	15.16		On the night 15/16 the front line Companies were relieved by the Companies in support and reserve, 'C' Coy relieving 'B', 'B' Coy coming into support; 'A' Coy into reserve. The relief was carried out without incident and there was no Casualties.	
	17		Nothing to report.	
	18-19		The Brigade line was re-distributed, the Battalion taking over the front line and support Posts from the 16th SUFFOLKS, Slightly readjusting its front to the right to the CALONNE-ROEBECQ ROAD inclusive. At the same time the 15th SUFFOLKS took over 7 posts in the rear line held by the Battalion. The re-distribution was carried out without incident or casualties.	
	20		Nothing to report.	
	21-22		On the night 21/22 a raid was carried out on enemy lines and surroundings in about Q.8.C.8.5. by a raiding party consisting of 20 O.Rs 'D' Coy under the command of 2/Lt R.J.T. WEBBER. The raid was carried out most skilfully, co-operation and was completely successful. The enemy line being entered and 3 unwounded prisoners being brought away affording valuable identifications. Casualties to raiding party 2 wounded.	

Army Form C. 2118.

WAR DIARY
or
INTELLIGENCE SUMMARY.
(Erase heading not required.)

Instructions regarding War Diaries and Intelligence Summaries are contained in F. S. Regs., Part II. and the Staff Manual respectively. Title pages will be prepared in manuscript.

Place	Date	Hour	Summary of Events and Information	Remarks and references to Appendices
IN THE LINE	July 23-24		On the night 23/24 the Battalion was relieved by the 16th (Yeomanry) Battalion DEVON REGIMENT and moved with remainder of the Brigade into Divisional Reserve, the Battalion billeting at GUARBECQUE. The relief was decidedly known to the enemy who heavily shelled the area during the relief with H.E. and gas. Battalion HQ at LES AMUSOIRES especially being heavily shelled from 12 m.d.night to 2 a.m. The relief was however completed with only 10 casualties to the 16. the 13 Battalion. This period was spent in refitting and training.	
GUARBECQUE	24/31		GENERAL NOTES	
			Health of the troops - The outbreak of 3 day fever continued at the commencement of the month, declined during the second week and disappeared entirely during the third and fourth weeks, the health of the troops during the latter end of the month being good	
			STRENGTH O/Rs 37 ORs 936.	
			REINFORCEMENTS O/Rs 3 ORs 39	
			CASUALTIES O/Rs killed Nil. wounded 1 (2/Lt C.T.BASS. Sx Yeo)	
			ORs killed 2. wounded 17	

Ref. Map FRANCE Sheet 36a. 1/40,000

Capt & Adjutant
YEOMANRY BATT.
Royal Sussex Regiment

WAR DIARY or INTELLIGENCE SUMMARY

Army Form C. 2118.

16 R Sussex R.

Map Refce FRANCE 36ª SE & NE 1/20,000

Place	Date	Hour	Summary of Events and Information	Remarks and references to Appendices
Guarbecque	1-4th		76 Brigade continued in Divisional Reserve and the Battalion was employed in training.	
	4th		On the night 4/5th the Battalion relieved the 2/5 R.W.F. in the Line in the Left subsector of the ST FLORIS Sector.	
			A Coy (Capt LASCELLES) in the FRONT LINE
B Coy (Lt A Adams)
C Coy (Lt E.G.S EDWARDS) } in the RESERVE LINE
D Coy (Lt W LOCKETT) in the AMUSOIRES – HAVERSKERQUE LINE
BATTALION HQ at P5c 2.9.
Relief quiet – no casualties.	
In the Line	5th & 6th		In the Line – no incident.	
	7th	6.20pm	Information received from the Division on the right that the enemy was withdrawing – the "Division" ordered to advance and occupy evacuated trenches. Orders received that the Batt^n would advance at 8.30pm. 1st Objective being enemy trenches across OLD RIVER LYS from K31 & 10.2 to K2 2 5.1. Left of A Coy was held up by River Lys for a considerable time, all bridges having been destroyed by the enemy except one which was maintaining touch and keeping direction.	
	8th		By this time the Bridging Coy (A Coy) were across the river. Temporary bridges having been constructed by REs and were notching a Clane astride the OLD RIVER LYS, CORNET MALO influence, all were in touch with 10th Buffs on the right. Lt Taylor was wounded. During the night and subsequently shortly of wounds.	
		5.40am	C Coy ordered to advanced through A Coy so far as the line drawn from South from Jury to K32 central and to consolidate this line as far as the OLD RIVER LYS. B Coy were ordered at the same time, to advance on the right of C Coy to continue their line North East with the BUFFS.	
		am	These men were carried out by 7.30 am. B & D Coy ordered to advance to line of OLD RIVER LYS from Q3 4.2.9 to K33 4.3.2. C Coy to remain in present position and consolidate. A Coy to consolidate in Palaires Groupe in approximate position. Batt HQ remained forward to East end of ST FLORIS. Posns .... opposition except from scattered M.G. from from ricks of OLD RIVER LYS.	

Army Form C. 2118.

WAR DIARY
or
INTELLIGENCE SUMMARY.

(Erase heading not required.)

Instructions regarding War Diaries and Intelligence Summaries are contained in F.S. Regs., Part II and the Staff Manual respectively. Title pages will be prepared in manuscript.

Map Ref.ce. FRANCE. 36" S.E & N.E. 1/20000

Place	Date 1916 AUGUST	Hour	Summary of Events and Information	Remarks and references to Appendices
Sh.h. Line	9th		During the early hours of the morning 3 bridges were thrown across the main trench Q.3 & 3.7 and R.33 d.2.1 & intermediate, established on the E. bank. 2/Lt WAUGH & 2/Lt R. Waugh & 1777 Pte SHORBENELL accompanied by Capt SPICKERNELL, saw an enemy M.G. Berlin moving forward to an already entrenched emplacement. He crawled out and the emplacement served and rushed it, capturing, however, the not running away. He brought the gunners in & returned to see what he could find. 2/Lt R WAUGH was awarded the M.C. & 1777 Pte SPICKERNELL W was awarded the M.M. for the act of gallantry.	
	10th		In the evening of the 10th/11th there was a relief/relaxation of the Divisional Bont. The relief front being held by 2nd/5th Brigade. The 10th/Dorset 31st Bn & D.R.Os. finding the front line and the 9th/Norf & support Lines. The relief/relaxation was carried out with little incident.	
	11,12,13		Battalion in support as ?...	
	14th		On the night of 14/15 the Battn relieved the 10th Dorsets in the left section of the Brigade front. A & C Coy. —front lnB (C.Coy was commanded by Capt A.BOSSER.) D Coy (now commanded by Capt WHO Armstrong) Rela. the front line assigned to (C Coy) taking the greater assignment to the Centre attack Coy in K.33 C.1.4 K.32 C.P.6 L/A Grace M.C	
	15th		In the lane - no incident.	
	16th		On the night 16/17 the Battn was relieved in the line by 2nd Bn RWF (23rd Brigade) and on relief went in to billets at HAMLET BILLET.	
HAMLET BILLET	17-24		Major A C Jones M.C. taken command of the Battn on the 18th inst & Col. A.H. POWELL EDWARDS to RAMPONNEAUX. During the period the Battn was employed - training.	
	24th		The Brigade was ordered in Divisional support by 25th Brigade and nov u/s Divisional Reserve. "C" Bass. Remover, remained in front billeting area commenced training.	
	25th		training covered.	
	26th		The Division was withdrawn from the line, the Battn moving to BOURECQ	
BOURECQ	27,28		Bn. Battn at BOURECQ.	
	29th		The Battn entrained at 9.40 p.m at HILLERS Station for HEILLY and killing fire.	
HEILLY	30th		At HEILLY awaiting orders.	

Army Form C. 2118.

WAR DIARY
or
INTELLIGENCE SUMMARY.
(Erase heading not required.)

Instructions regarding War Diaries and Intelligence Summaries are contained in F. S. Regs., Part II. and the Staff Manual respectively. Title pages will be prepared in manuscript.

Map Refce: FRANCE 36" SE & NE 1/20,000

Place	Date	Hour	Summary of Events and Information	Remarks and references to Appendices
HEILLY	31st		The Battalion received orders to embus at 4 p.m. and the intention of the Brigade shewing a Bugade of the 30th Division in Support in the line N.W. of PERONNE. On arrival at a point short of MARICOURT orders was received to leave the buses and march forward to a front E of MARICOURT where a guide would meet the Battalion. No other orders were received. The Battalion found the guide who she-led them himself and the Battalion arrived at 5 a.m. on the 1st Sept. The Battalion halted for the night in a field at about B 26 a 99 (Ref Pl FRANCE 62 a 1/40,000)	
			The health of the troops was good throughout the month.	
			Reinforcements offrs. 6 ORS. 20. Effective Strength offrs. 40 ORs 916.	

[signature]
Lieut. Colt.
YEOMANRY BATT
Royal Sussex Regiment

… Army Form C. 2118.

WAR DIARY
or
INTELLIGENCE SUMMARY.
(Erase heading not required)

Place	Date	Hour	Summary of Events and Information	Remarks and references to Appendices
HEM WOOD	Sept 1st		The Battalion arrived in the vicinity of HEM WOOD in the early hours of the morning after a very tiring march from the debussing point. In the evening, the C.O. was summoned to Bde. and given orders for the operations of the following day. The 74th Division, in conjunction with the Australian Division on the right, would attack at 5.30.am, the objective of the Division being the spurs W and SW of NURLU, and of the Australian Division, MIDINETTE TRENCH. Of the Division, the 229th Bde were to carry out the attack on a line S of MOISLAINS, with the 230th Bde, in support, and the 231st Bde in reserve. Within the 230th Bde, the Battn was to be disposed near the road junction in C.26 b, and 27. a., in readiness to move forward in close support. The SUFFOLKS and BUFFS in support and reserve to it. MAJOR A.C.SAYER.MC. was in command of the Battn, LT-COL EDWARDS remaining with "B" Teams for this tour of duty of the Battn.	
HEM WOOD	2nd.		The Battn moved out from bivouac at 2.45.am, and proceeded to the position of assembly, indicated above, which was reached at 5.25.am, the Battn being disposed in olds bits of trench and shell holes just as dawn was breaking. The 16th Devons (reserve Battn to 229th) were found on the same ground. Our barrage started at 5.30.am, and produced a fairly lively reply from the enemy, on to the area on which the Battn was lying, fortunately not causing many casualties. At 6.am, the 229th commenced to advance, and at 6.30am, the DEVONS moved on. At 7.35.am, the Battn was moved forward to keep in touch with the attack, and at 7.45, on receipt of a report to the effect that the Australians on the right were making good progress, had crossed the CANAL DU NORD, and were advancing up the opposite slopes to the PERONNE-NURLU Road, Major Sayer decided to advance the Battn on a two Company front to obtain touch with the Australian Division, and to seize and hold the approximate line AIZECOURT to junction of roads in C.20.b.0.5. Orders were consequently issued, and at 8.30am, the Battn moved off D.Company.(CAPT W-R-D.CUTHBERTSON) right front Company, B,Company (LT A.LUCAS.MC left front Company, D. Company to direct. C. Company (CAPT.A.R.EDWARDS) in close support, A, Company (CAPT E.H.POPE) in reserve, echeloned to left.- The Battn was very heavily shelled during the advance, particularly whilst crossing the CANAL DU NORD, but advanced with great steadiness as far as BRUNN TRENCH, SE of HAUTE ALLAINES. At 19am, no further advance having been observed from Battn HQ, the C.O. himself went forward to ascertain the position. On the way … personnel of the 229th Bde, were seen falling back NW of the Canal,	

Army Form C. 2118.

WAR DIARY
or
INTELLIGENCE SUMMARY.
(Erase heading not required.)

Place	Date	Hour	Summary of Events and Information	Remarks and references to Appendices
TRENCHES SE of HAUTE ALLAINES.	3rd.		and an Officer of the 229th, gave the information that the Bde had been heavily counter-attacked, and driven back from the objective, across the Canal, he with remnants of various Regiments proposed to hold SCUTARI TRENCH. At 19-45, the C.O. arrived at BRUNN TRENCH, and found the Battn disposed in it and neighbouring trenches, on the right of the Australians; the position was in direct view of the enemy gunners, and a fairly hot enfilade fire was maintained by them on the Battn, the Bde on the left having withdrawn, the left of the Battn was in the air. Further advance was out of the question, and the position as it was, was not a pleasant one. After consultation with the O.C. 27th Battn A.I.F. the C.O.moved two Companies, (B & C) to trenches a few hundred yards to the N, the left hand Company right back to the village of HAUTE ALLAINES, with the object of linking up as far as possible with the 229th in SCUTARI TRENCH, and of forming a defensive flank. This was done, but it was not possible to extend the left as far as SCUTARI TRENCH, and a large gap existed. The Battn lay in this position all day, under direct observation of the enemy. All movement was observed and shelled, and communication to the rear (runner only) was very difficult. At 5.30 pm, that evening, a Company of the SUFFOLKS reported on the Battn left, and closed the gap between it and the 229th. The night was spent expecting a counter-attack, which as a matter of fact, never came off. Casualties for the 2nd, were 3 Officers wounded, 12 other ranks killed, and 35 wounded. The Battn remained holding the above position throughout the day. During the morning, on receipt of a report from Bde, that the enemy were retiring, two Officers Patrols were sent out, one from B Company, under 2/LT,R.WAUGH.MC. and one from C. Company under 2/LT.OVENDEN. Both these patrols were fired on both by artillery and machine guns, very soon after they left the trench, but pushed on with great determination to obtain definite information, until 2/LT WAUGH was severely wounded, and of 2/LT OVENDEN's patrol, of 3 men, 2 were wounded. The patrols then withdrew with very tangible proof that the enemy was still there All wounded were got in, and the affair reflected very great credit on all who took part in the patrols. During the afternoon, a 5.9 shell burst in the dug-out, in which was CAPT.T.A.R.EDWARDS and (C Company) and several men. Two of the men were severely wounded, and the dug-out wrecked, but Capt Edwards was unhurt, except for a very severe shock,, which necessitated him handing over the Coy to	

Army Form C. 2118.

WAR DIARY
of
INTELLIGENCE SUMMARY.
(Erase heading not required.)

Instructions regarding War Diaries and Intelligence Summaries are contained in F.S. Regs., Part II. and the Staff Manual respectively. Title pages will be prepared in manuscript.

Place	Date	Hour	Summary of Events and Information	Remarks and references to Appendices
TRENCHES SE of HAUTE ALLAINES	4th.		2/LT Ovenden. At 1.am, the Australian Division, having pushed forward, in conjunction with an advance by the 231st Bde (74th Div) on the left, the Battn was withdrawn to bivouac in C.26,a &c.	
In bivouac at C.26,a & c.	5th.		During the morning, orders were received that the Battn must be prepared to move, the Battn having been allotted the duty of advance guard to the Division in the BDE pursuance of the enemy, who were now retiring Eastwards. At 2.15 pm. definite orders to move to D.25,c. in reserve to SUFFOLKS And BUFFS, were received, and at 3pm, the Battn moved off to this destination, which was reached at 4.45 pm. Some shelling was experienced on the way to this new position, and after arrival at it. There was little cover on the open slopes, but the Battn lay down in artillery formation, and had very few casualties. Patrols were pushed, out and liaison established with SUFFOLKS and BUFFS. During the night, two Companies were moved into MIDINETTE TRENCH, and two Companies were pushed forward to D.27,a & c. to act as support to advanced Battn, and deal with any counter-attack from direction of DRIENCOURT.	
AIZECOURT D.26,c.	6th.		At 11am, verbal orders were received from BGC, 230th Inf Bde, to occupy TEMPLEUX TRENCH with two Companies, and to keep the country to the NE under observation. A. & D. Companies were therefore ordered forward, C. & D. Companies advancing in support to them, and the above dispositions taken up. the BUFFS moving forward as the Battn came up behind. At 8pm, the Battn moved to the vicinity of TEMPLEUX LA FOSSE, and then took up a defensive position for the night. Two men of B. Company were badly wounded, by the explosion of a booby trap in an old trench, during the night.	
TEMPLEUX LA FOSSE.	7th.		At 9am, orders were received to move, out forthwith, and form a defensive flank on the N of the 231st Bde, who were to continue the advance. The Battn accordingly moved out via LONGAVESNES, B. Company to occupy high ground in E.21.d, and C. Company, new commanded by CAPT. FLETCHER, in E.21,b, which ground commanded a view to the north. Although itself, open to heavy shelling from that direction, A & D Companies were kept in hand at E.26,b, where also	

WAR DIARY
or
INTELLIGENCE SUMMARY.
(Erase heading not required)

Army Form C. 2118.

Place	Date	Hour	Summary of Events and Information	Remarks and references to Appendices
E. 26.b.	8th & 9th		Battn HQ were established. The Battn was again subjected to considerable shelling on its way to these positions, one unlucky shell falling amongst Battn HQ, and knocking out 5 Signallers and 2 runners. As soon as the above positions were reached, liaison was established with the attacking Battns of the 231st Bde and there being no need for the formation of a defensive flank, the Battn remain disposed of as above throughout the day, until the evening, when the Bde passed into Div reserve. The Battn remained where it was, B & C Companies were called in and all bivouaced in E.26.b. Battn HQ, in a small quarry in that square.	
E. 26.b.	10th		The Battn rested. At 5.10 pm, orders were received that the Battn would take over the portion of the front line, now held by the 16th DEVONS, and would have the BUFFS on the left, the SUFFOLKS being in Bde reserve. Information had been received earlier in the day that this relief would take place, and liaison had been established with the DEVONS and routes reconnoitred. At 7.30 pm, the Battn moved out of bivouac and at 8 pm, arrived at SPUR QUARRY, which was the HQ of the Devons, the whole relief was completed by midnight. Three Companies in the line, B, A, & C. in reserve, D. Coy, being as follows. under bank in K.5.b, 2,3, Each front line Company held a counter-attacking platoon in reserve. The front line held by the Battn ran from L.1.c.5.5. where it joined up with the Australians to F.19.d.3.5. where it joined the BUFFS. Battn HQ, in SPUR QUARRY.	
SPUR QUARRY	11th		The C.O. (Major A.C.Sayer. MC.) having looked at the ground in daylight, decided to reorganise the defence, and in accordance with his orders, A. Company was withdrawn from the line, which was now held by two Companies, B, on right and C, on left, with A, and D, Companies dug in, in platoon groups, in support, in K.6. a & b, and E. 30, a,b, & d, respectively.	
SPUR QUARRY	12th		Patrolling was vigorously carried out by day and night, and on this night a trap was laid for a party of the enemy, who were suspected of having a night post in BOULEAUX WOOD No 2, F. 26.b. Corporal DOWLING of B, Company, with 6 men, and a Lewis Gun, went out at dusk, and laid up for them: shortly after they got there, some 20 of the enemy appeared, the Lewis gun opened fire on them	

WAR DIARY
or
INTELLIGENCE SUMMARY.

(Erase heading not required.)

Army Form C. 2118.

Place	Date	Hour	Summary of Events and Information	Remarks and references to Appendices
SPUR QUARRY	13th		but jammed at the 3rd round, and the Bosche endeavoured to rush the party. Cpl Dowling, and one man, however, kept them off with bombs, while the gun, which was hopelessly jammed was withdrawn. They then got back themselves, and though not successful, this was a very gallant little affair.	
SPUR QUARRY	14th		No incident marked this day, except that in the evening, an enemy airman came down in a parachute, from a burning aeroplane, landed badly wounded in No Man's Land, and was brought in by C. Company. The Divisional dispositions were altered, and the Divl. front was re-distributed to be held by two Bdes instead of one, the 231st Bde taking over the left sector, and the 230th, the right. Of the Bde, the Battn continued to hold the NORTHERN SECTOR, with the SUFFOLKS on the right, between it and the Australians. At the same time, the Companies in the line were relieved, A & D taking over the front line, C Company coming into support, and B, to reserve in railway cutting immediately E of SPUR QUARRY. This was a most unfortunate night for B Company, for after being relieved, and whilst they were getting themselves into this cutting, the enemy heavily shelled the area, their 5.9's falling right among the Company, killing 4, and wounding 17 other ranks. The Company was therefore moved out of the cutting, and brought into SPUR QUARRY, which in turn, got shelled rather badly.	
SPUR QUARRY	15th		The enemy continued to shell the area heavily, and at 1.30 a.m. Major Sayer, MC, (who had commanded the Battn throughout operations from Sept 1st,) was wounded in the leg, and much against his will, sent down to the Dressing Station, Capt W.R.D.CUTHBERTSON, assuming command of the Battn.	
SPUR QUARRY	16th		Orders received for attack on the 18th. On this night the enemy heavily shelled the area with mustard gas, the bombardment lasting two hours. The whole area was contaminated with mustard gas, but as there was nowhere to move to, the Battn had to remain in the gassed area, and suffered a considerable number of casualties in consequence.	
SPUR QUARRY	17th		The day was passed in issuing orders, and making preparations for the attack on the 18th. In brief, the orders were as follows. The 74th Div, with the 1st Australian Division on the right, and the 58th Div, on the left, were to	

Army Form C. 2118.

WAR DIARY
or
INTELLIGENCE SUMMARY.
(Erase heading not required)

Place	Date	Hour	Summary of Events and Information	Remarks and references to Appendices
SPUR QUARRY.	Sept. 18th		attack and capture the enemy positions forward of the HINDENBURGH line in the Division, the 230 Bde would attack on the right and the 231st Bde on left each Bde had one Battn of the 229 Bde attached to it,- the SOMERSETS to the 230th & the DEVONS to the 231st Bde. Within the Bde, the SUFFOLKS on right & the Battn. on left were to attack and capture the GREEN LINE (first objective) namely, trench system from L.4.B.2.5. to F28.d.4.3. of this the Battn being responsible from F28.d.3.0. to TOINE WOOD F23.b.4.3. : i.e. CONNOR POST to TOINE POST both inclusive. The SUFFOLKS were to come at TEMPLEUX LE GUERARD from the S.E. leave two Coys, to mop it and the quarries up, and press on to first objective, the Battn was responsible for mopping up that portion of the large quarries which came in its area. The advance was to be made under cover of a creeping artillery & M.G. barrage. The SOMERSETS were to follow up behind the Battn. and the BUFFS behind the SUFFOLKS and the first objective being gained were to leapfrog over the two attacking Battns. and to continue the advance to the RED LINE (second objective) trench system in A25.d. F.30 C & A. to cross roads in F29. b.9.8. A subsequent line, BLUE LINE, known as the exploitation line was to be occupied if possible at any rate tactical points in it, this line was the line immediately in front of the HINDENBURG LINE comprising QUENNEMONT FARM, MALAKOFF WOOD, running through A26.d & b. ZERO hour was to be 5.20am. at which time attacking Battns. would be formed up closely behind the barrage line in front of our wire. This was roughly the general scheme: Within the Battn. "A"Coy. (Capt. Lascelles) were to attack on the right. "D"Coy. (Lt.West) on the left, "A"Coy. to direct, in support "C"Coy. (Capt. Fletcher) on right, "B"Coy. (Lt. Lucas M.C.) on left. All Coys., on a two platoon frontage the Battn in four waves. -	
SPUR QUARRY	Sept.18 th		At 2.45 am the Batt moved up to position of assembly, with the exception of A & D Coys who were holding front line and who had been responsible for gaps in our wire and taping the joining up line, Bn H.Q moved to front line trench at road in F25.c.9.0. At 5.20 our barrage started, at 5.23 it commenced to lift forward and the Battn advanced behind it to the attack.	

Army Form C. 2118.

WAR DIARY
or
INTELLIGENCE SUMMARY.
(Erase heading not required.)

Instructions regarding War Diaries and Intelligence Summaries are contained in F.S. Regs., Part II. and the Staff Manual respectively. Title pages will be prepared in manuscript.

Place	Date	Hour	Summary of Events and Information	Remarks and references to Appendices
SPUR QUARRY	Sept 18th		The morning was very dark and it was raining hard, in addition the smoke of our barrage destroyed what little visibility there was and in the early stages of attack it was impossible to see a man five yards away, this undoubtedly made it impossible for the enemy to know what was coming, but it also made it very hard for our troops to keep touch or direction means, runner included; it was therefore some time before any definate news as to how the attack was getting on could be obtained, but at 6.15am Battn H.Q. having moved to a garden in F26.d.2.4, our troops could be seen forming up the huge chalk mounds about the grannaries in F27.d and in point of fact the first objective was gained by 7.30am. Throughout the attack the barrage was extradinarily good and our troops followed so closely behind it that they were upon the enemy before they had time to recover; the chief difficulty lay in leading straight, especially during the early stages of the attack when the atmosphere could only be compared to a particularly dense London fog, the greatest credit is due to Capt. Lascelles (A Coy) who personally directed the advance and with extra-ordinary skill had the Battn on to its objective to a yard. Casualties were happily few, taking into consideration the length of the advance and the natural strength of the country over which the attack passed; on the other hand a large haul of prisoners was made, the Battn itself capturing between four and five hundred unwounded prisoners, beside many machine guns and trench mortars. In view of statements in the papers to the effect that"our troops went round the chalk quarries at TEMPLEUX LE GUERRARD under cover of smoke screens" it is interesting to note that Capt.Lascelles and about 15 men of A.Coy went straight up the side of the biggest mound, over the wire at the top in the face of some 70 enemy with machine guns the whole lot of whom they either killed or captured. The Battn remained on the first objective to consolidate, meanwhile the Batts in the rear passed through them and advanced on the RED LINE which they subsequently captured, it was not found possible to advance to the BLUE LINE. The Battn that night was disposed as follows,"A"Coy in CONNOR POST, "D"Coy in TOINE POST. "C" Coy dug in in support tom "A" and "B" in support to "D" Coy. H.Q. in SHERWOOD TRENCH F27.d.4.8.	

Army Form C. 2118.

WAR DIARY
or
INTELLIGENCE SUMMARY.
(Erase heading not required.)

Instructions regarding War Diaries and Intelligence Summaries are contained in F.S. Regs., Part II. and the Staff Manual respectively. Title pages will be prepared in manuscript.

Place	Date	Hour	Summary of Events and Information	Remarks and references to Appendices
			Casualties for the day:- Officers wounded Lt.Lucas M.C.& Lt.Skinner Other ranks. killed 5. wounded 43 missing 1. At 5.45 "C"Coy were moved forward to F29.b.1.5. with orders to keep in touch with SOMERSETS.	
SHERWOOD TRENCH	Sept.19th		Battn remained disposed as above throughout the day but in the evening took over the line from the BLACK WATCH & SOMERSETS in the left sector of the Bde front from from F30.c.1.9. to cross roads at F29.b.9.9. B & C Coys in the line. A Coy in support at ARTAXERXES post, D Coy in reserve in TEMPLEUX SWITCH. During the night orders were received to occupy the sunken road in front of our line in F30.a. accordingly patrols under two officers were sent forward backed up by Lewis Guns, who occupied the road subsequently digging in during the night. Battn H.Q were now at dug-outs in TEMPLEUX SWITCH.	
TEMPLEUX SWITCH	Sept.20th		During the afternoon orders were received from Bde ordering the resumption of the attack on the BLUE LINE. The direction of the attack to be in a NORTH EASTERLY direction, the Bde objective being trench line from K2a. A20.c.8.3. to A14.c.0.4.. the battn to attack on the left from A20.a.0.0 to Bde north boundary with the BUFFS on the right and the 231st Bde on the left. The SUFFOLKS in support. The attack to be carried out under a creeping barrage similar to that on the 18th. Orders were issued to Companies in accordanve C Coy to attack on the right B Coy on the left with A Coy in support and D Coy in reserve; the front line Companies to go straight to the objective. A Coy to send one platoon to follow the advance but if not required to reinforce, to establish itself in locality of QUENNETT LOW TRENCH (F30.a.). Battn H.Q. and R.A.P. to be at ARTAXERXES POST. The system of forming up behind barrage to be similar to that obtaining on the 18th. ZERO hour to be 5.40 a.m.	
TEMPLEUX SWITCH	Sept.21st		At 4.30. the reserve and support companies commenced to move forward to the forming up ground and at the same time Battn H.Q. moved up to ARTAXERXES POST, the enemy shell fire at this time was already fairly heavy amounting almost to "counter preparation" fire, especially on our front line: forming up however was carried out without any confusion	

WAR DIARY
or
INTELLIGENCE SUMMARY.
(Erase heading not required.)

Army Form C. 2118.

Instructions regarding War Diaries and Intelligence Summaries are contained in F. S. Regs., Part II. and the Staff Manual respectively. Title pages will be prepared in manuscript.

Place	Date	Hour	Summary of Events and Information	Remarks and references to Appendices
			but with several casualties Capt.Fletcher (O.C. "C" Coy directing company) being wounded a few minutes before ZERO hour. At 5.40.am. our barrage open and was immediately answered by a very heavy enemy barrage both on the front line and support lines, a heavy machine gun fire also opened on the advancing troops; from now onwards the enemy fire never slackened and was exceedingly heavy in all calibres. Communications at once went wrong, all wires being instantly cut and runners becoming casualties before they could deliver their messages. The attack proceeded steadily in the face of this fire but a large number of enemy machine guns were passed over and subsequently gave great trouble; our own barrage did not appear to be anything like so good as on the 19th. whereas enemy fire of all sorts was far more formidable. During the early stages of the advance troops on our left lost direction and swept across our front carrying the whole attack too far to the right and leaving the flank attack exposed. Elements of the two leading Companies actually reached the objective, but were too few to hold it and were forced back again to 200 trench, here A Coy under Capt. Lascelles had established themselves with D Coy on the left and various elements of the Bde on the left and here they remained from 6.30.am to midday, subjected to the heaviest possible enemy fire of all description from both flanks and even machine guns from the rear, from enemy machine guns that had been passed over in the advance, at midday being now reduced to a mere handfull and their being no available supports ready to come up the order was given to withdraw to the unken road from which the advance had started, to accomplish this withdrawal the remaining Lewis Guns had to be sacrificed to give covering fire and the survivors had to fight their way back. Casualties were very heavy, all Company Commanders being knocked out and only 3 Officers remaining in all companies. The Battn fought throughout with the greatest gallantry and innumerable cases of exceptional gallantry occured but very few witnesses remained to give evidence of them: throughout the whole engagement Capt.Lascelles himself wounded twice displayed the most admirable courage and self sacrifice, encouraging and controlling not only his own Company but remnants of others that he collected round him and subsequently organising and carrying out the withdrawal	

Army Form C. 2118

WAR DIARY
or
INTELLIGENCE SUMMARY
(Erase heading not required.)

Instructions regarding War Diaries and Intelligence Summaries are contained in F.S. Regs., Part II. and the Staff Manual respectively. Title Pages will be prepared in manuscript.

Place	Date	Hour	Summary of Events and Information	Remarks and references to Appendices
			of the remnants of the Battn. only going to the R.A.P. to have his wounds dressed when he had got his men back to our lines. This was a very bad day for the Battn. only three Officers & 31 O.R's got back to our lines in the first instance though several stragglers turned up later. The Battn. had gone into the fight weak and had fought magnificently for six hours against greatly superior numbers backed up by exceptionally heavy and well directed shell fire. In the evening the remnants of the Battn. were relieved and came out of the line, Companies occupying TEMPLEUX SWITCH and Battn. H.Q. TOINE POST.	
TOINE POST	Sept. 22nd		Battn. occupied line from CONNOR POST exclusive to TOINE POST inclusive, Battn. H.Q. moved to trenches in F28.a.7.2.	
	Sept. 23rd		Battn. H.Q. and two Coys. moved back into SHERWOOD TRENCH, two Coys. in trenches in F28.a.7.2.	
SHERWOOD TRENCH.	Sept. 24th		The Battn. with the division was relieved and marched to and went into bivouac near TEMPLEUX LE FOSSE.	
TEMPLEUX LE FOSSE.	Sept. 25th		Battn. marched to PERRONNE and then entrained to VILLERS BRETTONEUX whence it marched to and went into billet at FOUILLOY.	
FOUILLOY.	Sept. 26/27			
FOUILLOY	Sept. 28th		Battn. entrained at HEILLY for LILLERS whence it marched to and went into billets at L'ECLEME.	
FOUILLOY	Sept. 29th		Orders received that the Battn. would take over the line from a Battn. of the 19th Division on the night OCT. 1/2, thus being given no time either to re-organize or refit.	
FOUILLOY	Sept. 30th		Advanced party of Coy Commanders went up to the line to be taken over.	

Army Form C. 2118

WAR DIARY
or
INTELLIGENCE SUMMARY
(Erase heading not required.)

Place	Date	Hour	Summary of Events and Information	Remarks and references to Appendices
			EFFECTIVE STRENGTH of UNIT 30/9/18. OFFICERS 32. O.R's 566	
			REINFORCEMENTS during month. " 8 " 6	
			CASUALTIES for month.	
			OFFICERS. KILLED. 1.	
			WOUNDED. 14.	
			MISSING 3.	
			O.R's. KILLED 47.	
			SINCE DIED OF WOUNDS. 10.	
			WOUNDED 222.	
			(SHELL GAS) " 3.	
			-MISSING 50.	
			NOMINAL ROLL of OFFICER REINFORCEMENTS.	
			Lt. H. Tripp. R.Sx.R. 2/Lt. A.P-Shapland. R.SR	
			" N.H. Mount. Sx. Yeo. " W.J.Wright. "	
			2/Lt.D.H. Christie.R.Sx.R. " Papineau Sx. Y	
			" F. Goldring " " Baker. "	
			NOMINAL ROLL of OFFICER CASUALTIES.	
			KILLED. 2/Lt. D.H. Christie. R. Sx. R.	
			WOUNDED. Maj. A.C. Sayer. M.C. Sx. Yeo. 2/Lt. R. Waugh. M.C. R.Sx.R.
			Capt.F.W. Lascelles. " " S. Hoad. M.M. Sx. Yeo.
			" A. Fletcher. " " H.J.M. Sheen. R.Sx.R.
			Lieut. A. Lucas. M.C. Gen. List " C.H. Ovenden
			" H.F. Skinner. R.Sx.R. " W.E. Richards
			" J.T. Smith. Sx. Yeo.	
			" F.A. West. R.Sx.R.	
			2/ " E.E. Evershed. Sx. Yeo.	
			" C.A. Foster. "	
			WOUNDED. contd.	

WAR DIARY
or
INTELLIGENCE SUMMARY
(Erase heading not required.)

Army Form C. 2118

Instructions regarding War Diaries and Intelligence Summaries are contained in F. S. Regs., Part II. and the Staff Manual respectively. Title Pages will be prepared in manuscript.

Place	Date	Hour	Summary of Events and Information	Remarks and references to Appendices

			NOMINAL ROLL of OFFICER CASUALTIES. contd.
			 MISSING. Lieut. H. Trigg. R.Sx.R.
			             2/Lt. W. E. Thomas. "
			               " A. Boardman. "
			
			 Health of troops throughout month. GOOD.	

[signature]

Lt.Colonel.
Cmdg. Sussex Yeo. Battn.
ROYAL SUSSEX REGT.

1875 Wt. W593/826 1,000,000 4/15 J.B.C. & A. A.D.S.S./Forms/C. 2118.

16 Sussex

WAR DIARY
or
INTELLIGENCE SUMMARY.
(Erase heading not required.)

Army Form C. 2118.

Place	Date.	Hour	Summary of Events and Information	Remarks and references to Appendices
	1918. October.			
Le CLEME	1st.		Left Le Cleme for Richbourg Lavoue and Battalion proceeded to take over in the line from 9th Welch Regt.(19th Division) at 1600. — Relief completed by 2300.	
RICHBOURG	2nd.		Battalion advanced at 1435 and took the first objective,Satan Trench,S.12 a. by 1500. The advance continued and the Battalion took up a line on the Road from T.14.a.2.0. to T.2.d.8.7. reaching this line about 2000 - this was accomplished without casualties. The 10th Buffs were on our right and the 15th Suffolks on our left.	
HALPEGARBE	3rd.		At 0730 orders were received and the advance continued. The Battalion advanced to line of Railway from U.8.c.2.0. to U.7-b.8 and thence Northwards to East edge of wood in U.7.b.4.9. Battalion H.Q. were established at Le CuCQUERREZ Farm.	
Le CUCQUERREZ Farm	4th.		Orders were issued for the Battalion to go into Brigade Reserve. 15th Suffolks passing through,with 10th Buffs in support,to continue the advance on this & the Battalions front. The 15th Suffolks having passed through,their Battalion & established a line East of LATTRES at 1400,with their right flank being refused to conform with Brigade on right. Further advance of 15th Suffolks being held up, the Battalion was ordered to hold line U.13.b and U.7.d, as a Support line.	
-do-	5th		Quiet day-No advance was made by 15th Suffolks— The Battalion was employed in improving their accommodation.— 3 Companies billeting in village of SAINGHIN-en-wEPPES.	
-do-	6th.		Another quiet day— Battalion employed in the night, digging a new line of retention U.8.b & d. Owing to shell fire, "A" & "D" Companies were withdrawn to huts in CHATEAU WOOD in U.7.a & b.	
-do-	7th		The Battalion relieved the 10th Buffs in Support Line in U.8. b & d.	
-do-	8th.		Quiet day.	
-do-	9th		Quiet day— Enemy shelling increased during the night.— Casualties were,however quite slight.	

Army Form C. 2118

WAR DIARY
or
INTELLIGENCE SUMMARY
(Erase heading not required.)

Place	Date	Hour	Summary of Events and Information	Remarks and references to Appendices
Le COCQUEREL FARM	9th(cont)		Orders were received for the Battalion to take over a line held partly by 19th K.S.L.I. & 10th Buffs. and reconnoitreing was duly carried out by the Commanding Officer and Company Commanders.	Ref Sheet 36 1/40000
CHATEAU de la VALLEE.	10th		The relief was duly carried out by 1030 and the line then held by the Battalion running along railway from U.5.b.8.0. to U.5.b.7.6. thence N.W. through O.35.d.O.O. to road junction in O.34.b.9.4. Battalion H.Q. being established in Chateau de la Vallee. During this period active patrolling was carried out as reports were received that the enemy was about to retire.	
-do-	11th		Normal day- The left flank troubled by T.M. shelling. Heavy artillery informed who shelled the area in question with little result.	
-do-	12th		Lt.Col H.I.Powell Edwards (Sussex Yeomanry) handed over command of the Battalion to Major J.B.Dodge D.S.C. (Machine Gun Corps). Orders were received issued for plans for further forward movement to be submitted. A fighting patrol of 1 Officer & 11 men supported by an artillery barrage attempted a raid on the Western edge of LA HAIE Wood to obtain an identification but failed to achieve its objecti owing to scarcity of artillery support and concrete pill-box with 2 Machine Guns strongly held.	
-do-	13th		At 0510 the enemy put down a heavy barrage and attacked "A" Company's left hand post with a force of between 30 & 40 men. Under this barrage our post had to withdraw and afterwards reestablished themselves although every man had become a casualty. The situation was restored by 0600, the enemy failing to get any identification. Vigorous patrolling was carried out during the day and a patrol sent out at 1630 found trench East of Railway unoccupied and posts were established on a line running U.6.c.5.8.-U 6.a.2.6.-O 36.c.O.O-O 35 d.8.3 -O 35.d.6.3.-O 35.c.7.2.-O 35.c.5.8. Orders received that the 15th Suriolks would take over the line and the Battalion would go into reserve. Relief completed by 2300 and Battalion occupied huts vacated by 10th Buffs in Chateau grounds in N 7.a.& b.	
-do-	14th.		Quiet day- devoted to cleaning up and rest.	

Wt. W593/826 1,000,000 4/15 J.B.C. & A. A.D.S.S./Forms/C. 2118.

Army Form C. 2118

WAR DIARY
or
INTELLIGENCE SUMMARY
(Erase heading not required.)

3

Place	Date	Hour	Summary of Events and Information	Remarks and references to Appendices
CHATEAU de la VALLEE	15th		Information received that the enemy was preparing to withdraw. The Battalion to stand by ready to move at short notice. 47th Division received orders to continue advance next day and the Battalion moved up to position on Corps Line of resistance in U 2.b & O 32 d. Battalion H.Q. at FOURNES.	Ref Sheets 36, 37 1/40000
-do-	16th		Quiet day- Battalion being in Brigade Reserve.	
FLEQUIRIES	17th		Advance was continued and the Battalion was ordered to go forward and billet in SANTES Area. On arrival further orders were received to proceed via HARBOURDIN to FLEQUIERIES where the Battalion were billeted for the night and were withdrawn into Divisional Reserve. Battalion all in billets at 2100.	
RONCHIN	18th		The Battalion left FLEQUIRIES at 1330 en route for RONCHIN where it arrived at 1630 and billeted for the night.	
CHERENG	19th		Battalion left RONCHIN at 1700 and proceeded to CHERENG where they went into billets on arrival at 2000.	
CAMPHIN	20th		Battalion left CHARENG at 0900 for CAMPHIN arriving there at 1030 and went into billets.	
-do-	21st.		Training in Lewis Gunnery and Signalling started and general cleaning up and overhauling of kits &c took place.	
-do-	22nd		Quiet day- Training continued.	
-do-	23rd.		Orders to relieve the 12th Somerset Light Infantry at ORCQ received and reconnaissances made. Orders were subsequently cancelled.	
-do-	24th		230th Brigade relieved 229th Brigade in the Line. This Battalion relieving the 12th Somerset Light Infantry in Support and proceeded to MARQUAIN arriving there at 1730. 10th Buffs in the line 16th Sussex and 15th Suffolks in Support.	

Army Form C. 2118

WAR DIARY
or
INTELLIGENCE SUMMARY
(Erase heading not required.)

Instructions regarding War Diaries and Intelligence Summaries are contained in F. S. Regs., Part II. and the Staff Manual respectively. Title Pages will be prepared in manuscript.

Place	Date	Hour	Summary of Events and Information	Remarks and references to Appendices
MARQUAIN	25th.		Reconnaisance of area allotted as Line of Retention made by Commanding Officer and Company Commanders at 0530. Line of Retention running from O.25.d.2.O. O.25.b.2.O.-O.19.central v O.13 d.O.O. v O.13.a.5.O.of this. Sussex holding from O.19 central to O.13 a.5.O.with right being 15th Suffolks. Disposition of the Battalion wereas follows:- "C" Company on right,"A" Company on left, supported by "B" & "D" Coys respectively. Posts on these lines being subsequently dug in the night. "B" Teams arrived at Transport lines from Divisional Reception Camp and 44 reinforcements arrived with the Battalion from the same place.	Ref Sheet 37/1/4000
MARQUAIN	26.27.28th		Battalion in Support - Lewis Gun training and firing continued.	
MARQUAIN	28th		Battalion relieved 2 left Companies of Buffs in the line.	
-do-	29th		Gas barrage put down on one Company post - any casualties.	
-do-	30th		Battalion relieved by 24th WELSH . relief completed by 2200 and the Battalion went into billets at LEMAIN.	
LEMAIN.	31st		Day devoted to cleaning up generally.	
			----------------@------------------	
			The Health of the Troops remained.on the whole, good,throughout the month.	
			Reinforcements during the month Officers 9. O.Rks. 3.	
			Effective Strength of Battalion. Officers 30 O.Rks. 538.	

J.P.Stodey Lt.Col.
Commanding Sussex Yeomanry Bn
ROYAL SUSSEX REGT.

WAR DIARY

INTELLIGENCE SUMMARY

(Erase heading not required.)

Place	Date 1918 NOVEMBER	Hour	Summary of Events and Information	Remarks and references to Appendices
LAMAIN	1-3rd		Getting ready for new duties in TOURNAI- Time devoted mostly to cleaning and mending clothes, re-equipping etc.	
-do-	4th.		Battalion starting training in Ceremonial Drill, marching past &c. SSignalling class started.	
-do-	5th.		Inspection by Brigadier General Commanding postponed owing to bad weather.	
-do-	6th.		B.G.C. inspected the Battalion at 1100, and also presented ribbons to the recipients of the MM. "B" Teams joined the Battalion.	
-do-	7th.		Training continued- The Battalion placed under orders to move at 4 hours notice.	
-do-	8th.		Battalion moved at 0730 with the intention of entering TOURNAI but were stopped at MARQUAIN owing to the enemy still holding East bank of the River SCHELDT. Battalion returned to original billets in LAMAIN.	
-do-	9th.		Battalion marched to TOURNAI, at 0730 and picquetted the entrances to the Town from the South and South East. Battalion was billeted in the Infantry Barracks in the Southern outskirts of the Town, relieving the 13th KINGS.	
TOURNAI	10th.		Battalion continued it's picquet duties.	
-do-	11th.		Battalion received orders to move EASTWARD, being relieved by 20th LONDON Regiment. At 0900 news of the signing of the Armistice was received and the Battalion was ordered to stand fast, but subsequently, at 1130 marched Eastward to the villages of PIRE & MONTROEUIL au BOIS.	
MONTROEUL au BOIS.	12th.		Battalion continued the march Eastwards and to SARTIAU in the PIRONCHE area.	
SARTIAU	13th.		Training continued- 2 Companies a day working at cleaning and draining the roads.	

Army Form C. 2118.

WAR DIARY

INTELLIGENCE SUMMARY.

(Erase heading not required.)

Instructions regarding War Diaries and Intelligence Summaries are contained in F. S. Regs., Part II. and the Staff Manual respectively. Title pages will be prepared in manuscript.

Place	Date 1918. NOVEMBER.	Hour	Summary of Events and Information	Remarks and references to Appendices
Pironche	16th.		The Battalion marched to THIMOUGIES.	
THIMOUGIES	17th.		Special Church Parade for Thanksgiving Service.	
-do-	18th.		Battalion worked on Road Craters -- Half the Battalion working in the morning and half in the afternoon.	
-do-	19th.		The Commanding Office inspected half the Battalion.	
-do-	20th.		Remainder of the Battalion inspected by The Commanding Officer.	
-do-	21st-23rd.		Work on the Road Craters continued. Class of instruction for N.C.O's started.	
-do-	24th.		Church Parade Service in the morning. ~~~~~ Battalion innoculated (T.A.B.)	
-do-	25th.		Work on the road continued. N.C.O's class also continued.	
-do-	26th.		Work still continued on the Road - In the afternoon a Transport competition was held which included Turn-out-Harness - and Driving competitions.	
-do-	27th.		Work on the Road continued.	
-do-	28th.		Work on the road continued - In the afternoon, the Battalion attended a lecture by Lt.Col Dowling on "Civil employment after the War".	
-do-	29th.		Battalion continued working on the Road. The Commanding Officer inspected the N.C.O's class and was ~~~~ satisfied with the result of the Course.	
-do-	30th.		Battalion went on a Route March - distance about 5-6 miles, in the morning and worked on the Road in the afternoon.	

Army Form C. 2118.

WAR DIARY
or
INTELLIGENCE SUMMARY.
(Erase heading not required)

Instructions regarding War Diaries and Intelligence Summaries are contained in F. S. Regs., Part II. and the Staff Manual respectively. Title pages will be prepared in manuscript.

Place	Date	Hour	Summary of Events and Information	Remarks and references to Appendices
			During the Month the preliminaries of the Education Scheme were taken in hand and such particulars as were necessary were taken and registered.	
			An epidemic of influenza caused a larger percentage of men to be admitted to Field Ambulance, *than usual*.	
			Effective Strength. Officers 42 Other Ranks 732	
			Reinforcements. Officers 0 Other Ranks 248.	
			The weather was mostly very wet and cold throughout the month.	
			In the Field. B.E.F. November 30th 1918.	
			[signature] Captain & A/Adjutant. Sussex Yeomanry Battalion Royal Sussex Regiment.	

Army Form C. 2118.

WAR DIARY
INTELLIGENCE SUMMARY
(Erase heading not required.)

Instructions regarding War Diaries and Intelligence Summaries are contained in F. S. Regs., Part II. and the Staff Manual respectively. Title pages will be prepared in manuscript.

Place	Date	Hour	Summary of Events and Information	Remarks and references to Appendices
	1916. DECEMBER.			
THIMOUGIES.	1st.		Church Parade- Battalion received 2nd Innoculation for T-A-B.	
"	2nd.		Work continued on the Road Craters.	
"	3rd.		Work continued on the Road Craters.	
"	4th.		Half the Battalion went to Baths at Barry- the other half continued work on the Road Crater at THIMOUGIES.	
"	5th.		Half the Battalion worked on road repairs in the neighbourhood of MAULDE - the rest of the Battalion went to the Baths at Barry.	
"	6th.		The Road Craters being finished the Battalion was engaged in Ceremonial Drill and Recreational Training.	
"	7th.		The Battalion lined the Road near MANSART Station to greet the King on his visit to the III Corps.	
"	8th.		Battalion Church Parade.	
"	9th.		Battalion engaged in Drill & Recreational Training.	
"	10th.		Educational Classes started - French & Shorthand being well attended. The rest of the Battalion being engaged in helping local farmers in Agricultural Work. -pulling & casting sugar beets carrots etc.	

WAR DIARY
or
INTELLIGENCE SUMMARY.
(Erase heading not required.)

Army Form C. 2118.

Place	Date	Hour	Summary of Events and Information	Remarks and references to Appendices
THIMOUGIES	11th to 14th		Agricultural Work continued.	
"	15th.		The Battalion marched to FRASNES and billeted there for the night.	
FRASNES	16th.		March continued at 0900 to OGY and the Battalion arrived at this place at 1400 and stayed the night in billets in this village.	
OGY	17th		The Battalion continued the march to BIEVENE and arrived at 1300.	
BIEVENE	18th.		Battalion employed in cleaning up billets etc.	
"	19th to 24th.		Battalion engaged in Education and Recreational training.	
"	25th.		Xmas Day - The G.O.C. 74th (Yeomanry) Division ordered that no guards were to be mounted either this day or the next.	
"	26th			
"	27th.		The Battalion was engaged in Physical Training and Education.	
"	28th.		Battalion went for a short Route march. Educational Training continued,	
"	29th.		The Battalion Armourer commenced an inspection of the Arms of the Battn.	
"	29th.		Church Parade.	
"	30th		Battalion engaged in Physical Training and Education. The Armourer continued the inspection of the Arms of the Battalion.	
"	31st.		Battalion went on a Route march and was also engaged in Educational Training.	

Army Form C. 2118.

WAR DIARY
or
INTELLIGENCE SUMMARY.
(*Erase heading not required.*)

Instructions regarding War Diaries and Intelligence Summaries are contained in F. S. Regs., Part II, and the Staff Manual respectively. Title pages will be prepared in manuscript.

Place	Date	Hour	Summary of Events and Information	Remarks and references to Appendices
			The health of the Troops continued to be excellent during the Month which was, on the whole, wet and cold.	
			The Education Scheme was taken well in hand and approximately 33 1/3 % of the Battalion attended classes.	
			Effective Strength 43 Officers	
			732. Other Ranks.	
			Reinforcements. 2. Officers	
			28. Other Ranks.	
			J. Babidge. Lieut Col.	
			Commanding Sussex Yeo Battalion	
			ROYAL SUSSEX REGIMENT.	

Army Form C. 2118.

WAR DIARY
or
INTELLIGENCE SUMMARY.
(Erase heading not required.)

Instructions regarding War Diaries and Intelligence Summaries are contained in F. S. Regs., Part II. and the Staff Manual respectively. Title pages will be prepared in manuscript.

Place	Date	Hour	Summary of Events and Information	Remarks and references to Appendices
	1919 January.			
BIEVENE	1st to 31st.		The month passed without incident. 1 hour each weekday morning was spent in either physical training or close order drill. These were attended by all. In case of men engaged in Education no other parade was compulsory. From 1000 to 1200 each day was devoted to Educational classes which were attended by an average of 50% of the Battalion. Mr Robinson of Winchester College delivered two lectures on the 18th. Major A.C.Sayer MC from Divisional Headquarters and Major Ponsonby from 10th Buffs came over to deliver special lectures. The afternoons were mostly devoted to sports. The Battalion was engaged in playing off matches of the Battn Football League which was started some months ago and also the Brigade League. Two Cross Country runs were held during the month, but the weather towards the end of the month was very bad and consisted of heavy falls of snow which mitigated against outdoor sports to a large extent. A Boxing tournament was held to find talent for the Divisional Boxing Contest to be held next month. The Battalion was fortunate in having a good Theatre in the village, baths,	

Army Form C. 2118.

WAR DIARY
or
INTELLIGENCE SUMMARY.
(Erase heading not required.)

Place	Date	Hour	Summary of Events and Information	Remarks and references to Appendices
			and also good recreation rooms. Nearly every evening some form of entertainment was provided, such as Whist and Bridge Drives, Debating Societies The Battalion Concert Party showed three times during the month and visits were received from the Concert Parties of the following Units etc 230th Field Ambulance., 229th Field Ambulance., Divisional Concert Party and also the 10th Buffs Pantomime Party. These visits were greatly appreciated by the Battalion. On the whole, the monotony of country life in a Belgium Village was considerably relieved. Demobilisation has proceeded smoothly and 4 Officers and 212 Other Ranks were either despatched for dispersal or were retained in England for demobilisation The health of the Troops remained good throughout the month. Effective Strength:- Officers - 39 Other Ranks 528.	

[signature]
Captain & A/Ad
16th (Sx Yeo)
Royal Sussex Regiment

Army Form C. 2118.

WAR DIARY
or
INTELLIGENCE SUMMARY

(Erase heading not required.)

Instructions regarding War Diaries and Intelligence Summaries are contained in F. S. Regs., Part II. and the Staff Manual respectively. Title pages will be prepared in manuscript.

Place	Date	Hour	Summary of Events and Information	Remarks and references to Appendices
BIEVENE	1919. February. 1st to 22nd.		The Battalion continued Educational Training in the mornings in addition to Physical Training, as per last month. In the afternoons sports were continued as far as the weather conditions would allow, and also various forms of amusements were provided in the evenings, such as Whist & Bridge Drives Dancing, and Boxing. The Battalion Concert Party gave three concerts to the men of the Battalion during the month in addition to giving various concerts to The Buffs and at the 3rd Corps Concentration Camp. Owing to members of the Concert Party being demobilized and proceeding to the Army of Occupation, the party (named "THE SWEDES") has now broken up. On 20th, the Battalion sent 5 Officers and 150 Other Ranks to join the 17th Battn ROYAL SUSSEX REGIMENT thus providing a draft for the Army of Occupation, reducing the Battalion to a very small number.	
BIEVENE	23rd		Orders were received that the Battalion would move to GRAMMONT on 25th and preparations were made for the amalgamation of the Battalion into one Composite Company.	
BIEVENE	24th		The Battalion reorganized and now consists of one Composite Company with	

Army Form C. 2118.

WAR DIARY
or
INTELLIGENCE SUMMARY
(Erase heading not required.)

Instructions regarding War Diaries and Intelligence Summaries are contained in F. S. Regs., Part II, and the Staff Manual respectively. Title pages will be prepared in manuscript.

Place	Date	Hour	Summary of Events and Information	Remarks and references to Appendices
ELVERNE	24th		Capt C.E.W.Price in Command. On the afternoon Orders were received that the move to GRAMMONT was postponed until 27th.	
"	25th & 26th		Owing to a draft being sent for Demobilization the Battalion became reduced to under strength of Cadre "B".	
"	27th		The Battalion moved to GRAMMONT and the move was completed satisfactorily, notwithstanding the small numbers remaining with the Battalion.	
GRAMMONT	28th		The Battalion was engaged in organization of billets and Stores etc. Owing to the death of the A/Adjt (Capt H.E.Blunt MC) on 16th while in Hospital Capt E.G.S.Edwards was appointed A/Adjutant. The health of the Troops was good during the month. The weather was not very good owing to snow and rain. Effective Strength:- Officers 29. Other Ranks. 139.	

P. Edwards.
Capt & A/Adjt.
16th (Sussex Yeo) Bn.
ROYAL SUSSEX REGIMENT.

GRAMMONT.

16th Surrey Rfls

Army Form C. 2118.

MARCH 1919

WAR DIARY
or
INTELLIGENCE SUMMARY.
(Erase heading not required.)

Place	Date	Hour	Summary of Events and Information	Remarks and references to Appendices
	1			
	2		Ordinary Parade	
	3		Orders received distributing Bn thr'oughout	
	4			
	5			
	6		The storing of weapons, stores & equipment that required transport in readiness	
	17		Painting Ordnance Stores from other units	
	18		Packing the men as they were to depart to [illegible] on closed trucks, eat	
	19		The Officer and men of the 1st route departure to join the South Federation [illegible]	
	20		on the Army of [illegible]	
	21		Second Party left England to dut. in draft enduring Cheer was sea	
	22			
	23		Orders for demobilisation	
	24		Same orders & later orders for cadre to UK for demobilisation	
	25		The remainder of O's cheque to demobilisation (inc) for UK	£22
	26			
	27		All Rams were received in actuality in same section on board for master to UK	
	28			
	29		Return of Rs "CADRE"	
	30		Arrived Purfleet	

Instructions regarding War Diaries and Intelligence Summaries are contained in F. S. Regs., Part II. and the Staff Manual respectively. Title pages will be prepared in manuscript.

WAR DIARY
or
~~INTELLIGENCE SUMMARY.~~
(Erase heading not required.)

Army Form C. 2118.

Place	Date	Hour	Summary of Events and Information	Remarks and references to Appendices
	31st		The [illegible] above the [illegible] [illegible]	
			[illegible] the 4th Battn Royal Sussex Regt. [illegible] Army of Occupation.	
			The unit is now (with the exception of 2 [illegible] officers) at [illegible] (which [illegible]	
			[illegible] to provide against [illegible])	
			[illegible] was [illegible] in the air.	
			Four [illegible] took place during the month as follows:	
			13th v 10th Buffs. 14th v 15th Suffolks. 15th 10th Buffs. 26th 10th KSLI	
			The health of the [illegible] the month has been good, there being only one man, [illegible]	
			to FA, (the remaining [illegible] days suffering from a slight cold.)	
			Instructions as to [illegible] have been [illegible]	
			[illegible]) owing to an epidemic among the [illegible] population.	
Grammont 1-4-19				

YEOMANRY BATT.
Royal Sussex Regiment

D. D. & L., London, E.C. (A7853) Wt W809/M1672 50,000 4/17 Sch 52a Forms/C/2118/14

Army Form C. 2118.

WAR DIARY
or
INTELLIGENCE SUMMARY.
(Erase heading not required.)

16 R Sussex
WO/1C/3

£23

Instructions regarding War Diaries and Intelligence Summaries are contained in F. S. Regs., Part II. and the Staff Manual respectively. Title pages will be prepared in manuscript.

Place	Date	Hour	Summary of Events and Information	Remarks and references to Appendices
GRAMMONT. BELGIUM.	1/4/19 to 30/4/19		The Padre engaged in general work preparatory to embarking to United Kingdom, such as cleaning, disinfecting and sacking all harness saddlery and general Mobilization stores. Vehicles have been cleaned, overhauled and oiled. The remainder of the animals were sent for demobilization on 25/4/19 pleasure trips were arranged for the troops to visit places of interest. The health of the troops throughout the month has been excellent.	

Lieut &A/Adjt.
Sussex Yeo Battn
Royal Sussex Regt.

Army Form C. 2118.

WAR DIARY
or
INTELLIGENCE SUMMARY.

(Erase heading not required.)

Place	Date	Hour	Summary of Events and Information	Remarks and references to Appendices
CHAMONT BELGIUM			The Cadre remained billeted in Chaumont throughout the month.	
			Nine other ranks were despatched for demobilization on the 5th.	
			and One Officer on the 21st, following an order for the reduction of the Cadre to 4 officers and 30 men.	
			Sports and entertainments were organized and arrangements made for troops to visit places of interest, such as Ostend, Waterloo, and Bruges. Five other ranks proceeded on 14 days leave to the United Kingdom during the month.	
			The health of the troops was good.	

[signature]

Lieut & A/Adjt.
for O.C. Sussex Yeo Battn.
ROYAL SUSSEX REGT.

www.ingramcontent.com/pod-product-compliance
Lightning Source LLC
Chambersburg PA
CBHW081458160426
43193CB00013B/2529